Pebble® Plus

Working Scientifically

USING FACTS AND INVESTIGATING

by Riley Flynn

raintree
a Capstone company — publishers for children

Raintree is an imprint of Capstone Global Library Limited, a company incorporated in England and Wales
having its registered office at 264 Banbury Road, Oxford, OX2 7DY – Registered company number: 6695582

www.raintree.co.uk
myorders@raintree.co.uk

Edited by Anna Butzer
Designed by Sarah Bennett
Picture research by Eric Gohl
Production by Laura Manthe

ISBN 978 1 4747 2258 2 (hardback)
20 19 18 17 16
10 9 8 7 6 5 4 3 2 1

ISBN 978 1 4747 2282 7 (paperback)
21 20 19 18 17
10 9 8 7 6 5 4 3 2 1

British Library Cataloguing in Publication Data
A full catalogue record for this book is available from the British Library.

Acknowledgements
iStockphoto: Christopher Futcher, 11, Gertjan_Ketelaars, 7, Marilyn Nieves, 9, Nicolefoto, 17; Shutterstock: ffolas,
15, Lehrer, 5, parinyabinsuk, cover, Trofimov Denis, 13, wavebreakmedia, 19, Yuri Samsonov, 20
Design Elements: Shutterstock

Printed and bound in the United Kingdom.

Contents

What are facts?

You need to write a report about honey bees. How are you going to do it? You need to gather facts and conduct an investigation.

5

What is a fact? A fact is a piece of information that we know is true. Bees live in hives. They have six legs. These are facts.

What is an investigation?

An investigation is like a test. We investigate to find answers to a question. An investigation can solve a problem.

An engineer uses investigations to test designs. A scientist uses investigations to answer questions. You can conduct investigations like a scientist to gather facts.

Facts from experiments

Let's experiment! An experiment is an investigation that can help you to discover facts. Think of a question. What attracts bees?

You predict that sweet things attract bees. You pour water into two bowls, and add sugar to one bowl. You observe that bees like the sweet water. Your prediction was correct!

Record and review the facts

Next you need to record all the facts. Three bees landed on the bowl of sweet water. You write this down and draw a picture. A picture can record a fact too.

You may gather a lot of facts.

Do you need to use them all?

You review your facts and

choose the best ones. Using

good facts makes a good report.

Let's investigate

Which spilled liquid will dry faster?
Make a prediction. Then find out!

What you need:

- 60 millilitres water
- 60 millilitres apple juice
- 60 millilitres fizzy drink
- chalk
- timer, clock or watch
- a friend to help you

What to do:

1. Find a sunny spot in the school playground or on a garden path.

2. Pour each liquid onto the path. Make sure you leave space between each liquid.

3. Draw a circle around the edges of each spilled liquid. Write the liquid's name below the circle. Begin the timer.

4. Observe the results. How long did it take each liquid to dry? Write the time in minutes.

5. Which liquid dried (evaporated) first?

What do you think now?

Make a claim. A claim is something you believe to be true. Why do you think one liquid dried faster than the others?

Glossary

engineer person who uses science and maths to plan, design or build

experiment scientific test to find out how something works

gather collect things

investigate search for facts to solve a problem or answer a question

observe watch someone or something closely in order to learn something

predict say what you think will happen in the future

problem something that raises questions

review study or look at again

Read more

The Big Book of Science: Things to Make and Do (Usborne Activities), Rebecca Gilpin (Usborne Publishing, 2012)

Experiments with Light (Read and Experiment), Isabel Thomas (Raintree, 2015)

Websites

www.bbc.co.uk/bitesize/ks1/science
Enjoy some fun activities and learn more about science.

www.dkfindout.com/uk/science
Find out more about science and famous scientists.

Comprehension questions

1. What is an investigation?

2. Describe a time when you needed to gather facts to answer a question.

Index